This gift is for:

_____

Who was baptized on:

_____

In the blessed location of:

_____

And is deeply loved by:

_____

"There is one Lord, one faith, one baptism;
there is one God and Father of all people, who
is Lord of all, works through all, and is in all."

—*Ephesians 4:5–6, GNT*

Celebrating My Baptism

THE DAY I JOINED GOD'S FAMILY

Illustrated by Estelle Corke

PARACLETE PRESS

"Let the little children come to me."

—*Mark 10:14, NRSVCE*

The Gift of Baptism

Baptism means to be
dipped in water.

Baptism is a symbol of
being made clean.

Water makes things
clean and strong
and full of life.

Baptism makes
my heart clean,
my faith strong,
and promises me
eternal life!

God's forgiveness
flows over me just like
the baptism water that
flows over my head.

With water and faith,
baptism tells everyone,
"Jesus died for me.
I have been made new!
I am part of God's family."

I am loved!

God the Creator sees *me*.

I am loved!

Jesus, God's Son, knows *me*.

I am loved!

Holy Spirit, God's helper, teaches *me*.

The Holy Trinity

Praise God, from whom all blessings flow;

Praise Him, all creatures here below;

Praise Him above, ye heavenly host:

Praise Father, Son, and Holy Ghost.

—Thomas Ken, 1674

The Trinity is three persons:
God the Father,
Jesus the Son,
and the Holy Spirit.

Jesus came from Nazareth of Galilee and was baptized by John in the Jordan. And just as he was coming up out of the water, he saw the heavens torn apart and the Spirit descending like a dove on him. And a voice came from heaven, "You are my Son, the Beloved; with you I am well pleased."

—*Mark 1:9–11, NRSVCE*

I adore the Trinity.

I love Jesus, he loves me.

God the Father all the time.

I am his, and he is mine.

Spirit, guide me every day.

I am deeply loved! Hooray!

Let God be the King of your heart. Be baptized in the name of Jesus Christ and be forgiven. Receive the gift of the Holy Spirit.

—*based on Acts 2:38*

God the Father

Father God,
you are the King who rules everything.

There is no one greater than you.

You are strong and powerful;
you watch over all things.

You created the moon and the sun,
everyone including me.

You protect your children and will
never leave.

Your love surrounds me today, tomorrow,
and forever.

God has many names
listed in the Holy Bible.

Abba – Father

Jehovah Shalom – The Lord is Peace

Yahweh – Lord

"God is wise and powerful! Praise him forever and ever."

—*Daniel 2:20, GNT*

You, LORD, are my shepherd.

I will never be in need.

You let me rest in fields of green grass.

You lead me to streams of peaceful water,

and you refresh my life.

You are true to your name,

and you lead me along the right paths.

I may walk through valleys as dark as death,

but I won't be afraid.

You are with me,

and your shepherd's rod makes me feel safe.

You treat me to a feast, while my enemies watch.

You honor me as your guest,

and you fill my cup until it overflows.

Your kindness and love will always be

with me each day of my life,

and I will live forever in your house, LORD.

—Psalm 23 CEV

Jesus the Son

Jesus came to Earth,
    just like you and me,
a perfect baby boy,
    who wise men came to see.
As he learned God's lessons
    and grew to be so strong,
he was something special;
    he did nothing wrong.
Jesus asked the people
    to love with all their heart,
to accept him as their Savior,
    and this would be the start.
God shared his Son, his rescue plan—
    a way to make things right.
When we believe, we rejoice,
    for Jesus is our light!

Jesus is called different names in the Bible
to help us know him better.

Bread of Life
Good Shepherd
King of Kings
Lamb of God
Messiah
Prince of Peace

Then God gave Christ the highest place and honored his name above all others. So at the name of Jesus everyone will bow down.

—*Philippians 2:9–10a, CEV*

Jesus loves me, this I know
for the Bible tells me so.
Little ones to him belong;
they are weak, but he is strong.
Yes, Jesus loves me! Yes, Jesus loves me!
Yes, Jesus loves me! The Bible tells me so.

—*Anna Bartlett Warner, 1860*

For God so loved the world that he gave
his only Son, so that everyone who believes
in him may not perish but may have
eternal life.

—*John 3:16, NRSVCE*

The Holy Spirit

God has given us the Holy Spirit,

who fills our hearts with his love.

—*Romans 5:5b, CEV*

I am never alone.
The Holy Spirit goes with me
wherever I go.
The Holy Spirit protects me.
He comforts me, calms me,
and fills me with hope.

The Holy Spirit is given different names
in the Bible.

Comforter

Helper

Spirit of Life

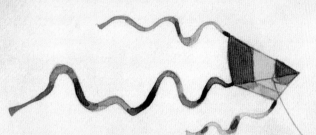

I turn away from doing wrong.
The Spirit helps me grow.

I ask for help to calm my fear.
The Spirit makes me whole.

I'm sad when things don't go my way.
The Spirit heals my soul.

"The fruit of the Spirit is love, joy, peace, patience, kindness, generosity, faithfulness, gentleness, and self-control. There is no law against such things."

—*Galatians 5:22–23, NRSVCE*

Me, A Child of God

"All of you are God's children because of
your faith in Christ Jesus."

—*Galatians 3:26, CEV*

Jesus loves the little children,

All the children of the world;

Red and yellow, black and white,

All are precious in His sight,

Jesus loves the little children of the world.

—*Clarence Herbert Woolston, late 1800s*

God's children have special names listed
in his Word.

Beloved
Disciple
Brother / Sister
Believer
Friend

The Spirit makes you God's children,
and by the Spirit's power we cry out to
God, "Father! My Father!"

—*Romans 8:15b, GNT*

The Lord's Prayer

Our Father who art in heaven,
hallowed be thy name;
thy kingdom come,
thy will be done
on earth, as it is in heaven.
Give us this day our daily bread,
and forgive us our trespasses,
as we forgive those who trespass against us;
and lead us not into temptation,
but deliver us from evil.

The Family of God

God's family is filled with people he loves
with all his heart.
These people may not look like one another.
They may not speak the same language.
But everyone praises the same Father,
believes in the same Savior, and walks with
the same Spirit.

Me and My Family

I am an individual
with my own tastes and gifts.
I'm special and exceptional
with my very own interests.

Although I am unique,
I share a unity
with my sisters and my brothers
in a kingdom family.

Let the water, cool and true,
be the sign that reminds you
your life is now completely new,
and you belong to Jesus, too.

For in the one Spirit we were all
baptized into one body.

—*1 Corinthians 12:13a, NRSVCE*

The Promise of Heaven

My hope, it is in heaven.
My future is secure.
I'll hug the Lord, Christ Jesus.
Yes, I am his for sure.

There won't be fear in heaven.
No hurts or pain or frowns.
My tears are wiped away,
God's tender love I've found.

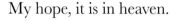

Thank you, Lord,
for loving us on earth
and in heaven. Amen.